Herbert Baynes, Dante Alighieri

Dante and his Ideal

Herbert Baynes, Dante Alighieri

Dante and his Ideal

ISBN/EAN: 9783743320383

Manufactured in Europe, USA, Canada, Australia, Japa

Cover: Foto ©ninafisch / pixelio.de

Manufactured and distributed by brebook publishing software (www.brebook.com)

Herbert Baynes, Dante Alighieri

Dante and his Ideal

DANTE AND HIS IDEAL

BY

HERBERT BAYNES, M.R.A.S.

Author of " Word-Pictures"
" The Evolution of Religious Thought in Modern India," etc.

WITH A FRONTISPIECE AFTER GIOTTO'S FRESCO.

London:
SWAN SONNENSCHEIN & CO.,
PATERNOSTER SQUARE.
1891

BUTLER & TANNER,
THE SELWOOD PRINTING WORKS,
FROME, AND LONDON.

PREFACE.

The object of this little book is twofold. On the one hand, it appeals to those who take delight in watching the growth of ideals, and more particularly in the fourteenth century; and, on the other, it endeavours to lay before the reader a consistent view of Dante's trilogy, according to the well-known theory of the late Dr. Karl Witte, which, in spite of all that has been said against it, seems to me the one most adequate to explain the facts.

As regards the poet's psychology, I am indebted to a very interesting article by Dr. Georg Simmel, which appeared in the *Zeitschrift für Sprachwissenschaft und Völkerpsychologie.*

Wherever translation appears in inverted commas, it is that of Professor Charles Tomlinson, F.R.S., the translator of the *Inferno;* in all other cases it is my own.

CONTENTS.

	PAGE
PREFACE	v
DANTE AND GOETHE	2
THE POET'S IDEAL	19
THE INFERNO	28
THE PURGATORIO AND THE POET'S PSYCHOLOGY	49
THE PARADISO	66
THE TRILOGY	75
BEATRICE AND THE SCIENCE DIVINE	88
APPENDIX	101

O voi, ch'avete gl'intelletti sani,
    Mirate la dottrina che s'asconde
    Sotto il velame degli versi strani.

O ye, who have the steady brain,
    Weigh well the thoughts which 'neath the veil
    Of mystic verses here remain!
                        —*Inf.* ix. 61.

DANTE AND HIS IDEAL.

In Dante it has been truly said, "ten silent centuries found a voice"; and for nearly six centuries the "mystic, unfathomable song" has been growing in favour, and has more than justified the name of its author—*Dante*, i.e. *Durante*, the enduring one, and *Allighieri*, the wing-bearer. His peculiar interest for our own day is this, that, though he was pre-eminently the Poet of Faith, he was the first to clearly enunciate the profound truth that we only arrive at Truth through Doubt. Indeed, I make bold to say, that he who will patiently listen to the singer of the fourteenth century will in the end learn more than from a study of the dramas and lyrics of him who is *par excellence* the poet of the nineteenth. Let us compare for a moment the masterpiece of the one with that of the other.

Alike in the *Divina Commedia* and in *Faust*, we have the description of a Pilgrim's Progress, and "from this world to that which is to come." Ideal creations as they both are, they are nevertheless as real as they are ideal. In the one case we have the revelation of the intense soul, Dante; in the other "the verbal expression of the essential man, Goethe." Much as we might like to have a glimpse into the childhood of

Dante and of Faust, the story of the earliest years is, nevertheless, for the most part left untold. When the veil is lifted we behold both pilgrims of middle age, in a state of profoundest gloom as regards both mind and life. The one can no longer live in the shows of things and feed upon the husks of the world. His country, his home, and even his most intimate friends, are filled with low desires and sordid ambition, and more especially with the three vices of Pride, Envy, and Avarice. He leaves the pleasant groves and calm retreats of what might have been the City of Peace, and all the association of years, and wanders forth an exile, shut out from his native shores. Thus it was, as pilgrim and stranger in the world of

Falsehood, the *selva oscura*, that he built himself, out of his own bosom, that edifice of undying Truth, home of the heart, broad on the roots of eternity. The other feels in the highest degree the woe of the world, the irony of life, and is more than "half in love with easeful death." A burden to himself and a mystery to his companions, he has but one wish left—to have done for ever with the stage on which he has played so impoten ta part. To the one this present world is but a passing show, an unreal shadow; so the theatre of his journeyings is "that awful other world," bodied forth in Hell, Purgatory, and Paradise. To the other it is "the world at large, as known to him, before whose calm intellectual vision had passed the long procession of the ages." Both pilgrims have their difficulties and dangers, and the latter his frequent falls; but for both there is redemption at last, and, even in heaven, a higher and more mysterious pilgrimage.

But we cannot fail to be struck with the great difference in the *moral* standpoint of the two men. To Goethe *sin* is after all a matter of no very great importance, and we are not a little astonished at the easy-going way in which, after a long life of manifold backsliding, Faust's immortal part is wafted to the skies. To Dante, on the other hand, all sin is of vital significance. To him the laureate's words apply :—

"The Poet in a golden clime was born,
With golden stars above;

Dowered with the hate of hate, the scorn of scorn,
The love of love!"

Banished from his native city whilst his country was torn asunder by faction and strife, his poet-heart bled for the suffering land, for the God-forsaken people; and as to St. John on that lonely isle of Patmos the vision of the New Jerusalem, so came to the banished Dante, in the stillness of noonday, whisperings of a higher and better life than any he had known. Then it was that he began to write that wonderful poem, the subject of which is man, the pilgrim, who, according to his actions, ascends the hill which leads to everlasting life or descends to "bottomless perdition."

Of Dante's biography little is known. He was born at Florence, near the monastery of Badia, where the Chiesa de' Bonomini now stands, on the 8th May, 1265. His father, Aldighiero II., died while the poet was still a boy; but his mother, Donna Bella, took care to give him the best education that was possible in those days. As his master, she chose Brunetto Latini, a well-known poet and philosopher, the *cotto aspetto* of the fifteenth canto of the *Inferno*. It was not long before Dante made himself master of several languages, and learnt to delight in *il suo maestro e il suo autore,* Virgil. Giving himself to the study of Aristotle and the classics, he soon became known among *color che sanno*. Astronomy, jurisprudence, medicine, geography, and geometry, were all included in his curriculum. His most intimate friend was the philosopher Guido Cavalcanti, whilst his guides in the fine arts were Giotto and Casella.

> " His Casella, whom he wooed to sing,
>   Met in the milder shades of Purgatory."

After wandering an exile in various places in Lombardy, Tuscany, and Romagna, he finally arrived at Ravenna, where he remained under the protection of the Signori da Polenta, until his death, on the 14th September, 1321, aged fifty-six.

But in order to fully realize the well-nigh impossible task which our poet set himself in undertaking to write the *Divine Comedy*, we must remember that the state of literature and of the scholar in the fourteenth century was such, that he who would own a copy of one or more of the few manuscripts which existed, must either himself spend months or perhaps years in careful transcription of the text, or, if sufficiently well-to-do, engage a professional scribe. The lot of the literary man in those days was anything but an enviable one. Some one applied to Petrarch for a copy of his treatise, *De Vita Solitaria*. His answer was:—

" God is my witness, that ten times and upwards I have endeavoured, if the style were not such as to give pleasure to the mind and the ear, that at least the written characters should please the eye; but all my attempts to overcome the well-known evasions of that part of the literary world known as the copyists have been vain. It may appear incredible that a work that required only a few months for its composition cannot be copied in as many years. After many delays, I left it as good as copied in the hands of a priest. I know not whether his promise will be held sacred, as befits his sacred character, or be as fallacious as that of a copyist."

The three earliest editions of the *Divina Commedia* appeared in the year 1472, the first at Foligno, the second at Jesi, and the third in Mantua. It is not a little remarkable that in none of these towns, not even in the home of that poet who was destined to lead Dante through Hell and Purgatory, has there ever appeared a second edition. Then follow Naples (1474), Venice

(1477), and Milan (1477-8). In Dante's native city, Florence, the first edition, with Landino's excellent commentary, appeared in 1481, followed by a second, with valuable woodcuts, in 1497. Then at long intervals came the editions of 1506, 1572, and 1595, of which the second only contains the *Inferno*, and it is worthy of remark, as characteristic of the age, that the two last describe the poet as a Florentine *nobleman*. After this we have a break of 176 years, and another of at least forty-one years. Since 1817, however, the Florentine press has, in this respect, been busier than that of any other city.

It is perhaps not too much to say that the state of Europe in the time of Dante was one of barbarism. The Church and the World were at open warfare, so that society was split into at least two factions, the Guelfs, or papal adherents, on the one hand, and the Ghibellines, or Imperialists, on the other. In these two parties all men were interested, for they disposed of the fortunes and lives of all. Being a well-known magistrate of Florence, where he was born, our poet was of course mixed up in these quarrels, and, indeed, became their victim. Now, this chaos of outer relations had its reflex in the spiritual life of those times. Pardons and indulgences were sold so as to be "adjusted to every vice" and to "take the place of every virtue." Long had the phantasy of Christendom been trying to realize the torments of the damned and the various forms of penance undergone by those who indeed had left the world in the faith, but with unexpiated guilt. Whilst reviving Art was representing the last judgment on church-doors and in mosaics, Literature was rich in visions of purgatory and the things beyond the grave. Nay, there was a more immediate sensuous representation of the fate of the disembodied spirit in the spiritual plays, and more especially the Easter plays, of France and Italy. The stage consisted of three stories, one above another. In the middle, one saw man and his dwelling-place, and the toil and turmoil of life. Above were the heavens and the persons of the Trinity, with angels and "spirits of the just made perfect"; but below were the fire and brimstone, and one could hear the oft-repeated cry, "Damnation ever; salvation never!" A most magnificent play of this kind was performed on one of the Florentine Arno-bridges in Dante's lifetime.[1] Nor is this to be wondered at. The daily increasing disasters of the time naturally led men to believe that the end of the world was at hand. Society had lost its ideals. Righteousness had given place to expediency. Hence the prophet of his age had to sing to eager listeners a message of awful grandeur, of life-long significance. He could not but show them the Hell in which they were living, the Purgatory through which, as he believed, it was possible for them to go, in order that, by repentance, they might reach

[1] See Karl Witte's *Göttliche Komödie*, p. 9.

the Paradise prepared for the redeemed. Cast forth by society, homeless, friendless, the poet sings his "mystic unfathomable song." As Carlyle grandly puts it:—

"The deeper naturally would the Eternal World impress itself on him; that awful reality over which, after all, this Time-world, with its Florences and banishments, only flutters as an unreal shadow. Florence thou shalt never see: but Hell and Purgatory and Heaven thou shalt surely see! What is Florence, CAN della Scala, and the World and Life altogether? Eternity: thither, of a truth, not elsewhither, art thou and all things bound! The great soul of Dante, homeless on earth, made its home more and more in that awful other world. Naturally his thoughts brooded on that, as on the one fact important for him. Bodied or bodiless, it is the one fact important for all men: but to Dante, in that age, it was bodied in fixed certainty of scientific shape; he no more doubted of that *Malebolge* Pool, that it all lay there with its gloomy circles, with its *alti guai,* and that he himself should see it, than we doubt that we should see Constantinople if we went thither. Dante's heart, long filled with this, brooding over it in speechless thought and awe, bursts forth at length into 'mystic, unfathomable song'; and this his *Divine Comedy,* the most remarkable of all modern Books, is the result."

When Dante began his great work,

and when he finished, it is not easy to determine. On the authority of Andrea di Leon Poggi, a nephew on the sister's side of our poet himself, Boccaccio tells us that he began it before the exile, and that at that time he had already composed the first seven canti. What seems to be pretty certain is, that the idea and the plan of the work were *anterior* to the exile, but that the execution was *posterior*.

Besides Italian verse, in which he was certainly most at home, the great Florentine wrote both poetry and prose in Latin. In prose we have *Monarchia*, a work full of the Ghibelline spirit, which was composed about the time when Arrigo VII. contemplated the subjugation of Italy, between 1312 and

1313, and a book entitled *De vulgari eloquentia*. A few eclogues and the beginning of a book in heroic verse are all that remain of Dante's attempt at Latin poetry.

Of his odes Leonardo Aretino well says:—

"Le canzone sue sono perfette e limate e leggiadre e piene d' alte sentenze, e tutte hanno generosi cominciamenti, siccome quella canzona che comincia:
Amor, che muovi tua virtù dal Cielo,
Come il Sol lo splendore;
Dove è comparazione filosofica e sottile intra gli effetti del Sole e gli effetti di amore. El' altra che comincia:
Tre donne intorno al cor mi son venute:
E l' altra che comincia.
Donne, che avete intelletto d' amore:
E cosi in molte altre canzone è sottile e limato e scientifico."

The experiences of his many-sided

life Dante has given us most systematically in the Latin treatise, *De Monarchia*, which is intimately connected with the *Divine Comedy*, and, together with his letters, forms the chief groundwork for the understanding of the poem. Amid all the distractions of the State, the feuds of parties, fights within and fears without, and the blatant intolerance of the Church, the poet saw no other way of making his nation free, united, and strong, than by placing it under the protection of a universal Emperor, who, supreme above all kings, princes, and dukes, free from all passions and parties, would administer justice and secure peace, the basis of a people's progress. This is clear, too, from a sonnet which was probably addressed to Arrigo VII., in which the Emperor is compared to the Holy Sepulchre of our Lord, whence cometh salvation :—

> Tornato è 'l sol, che la mia mente alberga,
>   E lo specchio degli occhi onde era ascoso,
>   Tornato è 'l sacro tempio e prezioso
> Sepolcro, che 'l mio core e l'alma terga.
>
> Ormai dal petto ogni vil nube sperga
>   Il ciel, che m' ha ridotto il dolce sposo.
>   Sorgete Muse, surga il glorioso
> Fonte, per cui tant' opra s'orna e verga.
>
> Ecco le stelle lagrimose e stanche,
>   Venuto a ritornare il caro segno,
>   Or fatte illustri, ecco la bella luce.
> O clemenza di Dio, potria morte anche
>
>   Scurare il sol ?—Nò signor mio benegno,
>   Questo è quel che impera, egli è mio duce.

And under the protection of a Church which, divested of all arrogance and deprived of all interference in worldly affairs, might the better watch over the spiritual well-being of her children.

According to the taste of his time, the prophet put his fundamental idea into the highest sphere of mysticism, and, in his visionary journey through Hell, Purgatory, and Paradise, made it manifest by means of a multitude of sublime pictures. There should be two equal framers and leaders of the world's-progress, responsible to God alone: namely, the Emperor, who by means of wise institutions, supported by the teachings of philosophers, should radiate gladness upon earth; and the Pope, who, according to the middle-age theory of revelation, would lead mankind to virtue and the true faith, and so make them worthy of heavenly blessedness.

So Dante chose for his mysterious pilgrimage two guides, Virgil, the singer of the Romans, who, in his epic, had glorified the holy Roman Empire and the first Emperor Augustus, and Beatrice, the poet's early love and here the symbol of Divine love and revelation. Hence Virgil is only at home in all that concerns mundane matters and the Empire generally, and in going through the Inferno shows his pupil Dante all the sad results of lawlessness, of rejection of the Divine will, of tyranny and greed; in short, of all the sins which hinder the peaceful and orderly development of the human race. In the Purgatorio are represented in various gradations the means of grace and of repentance, which God through the

Church vouchsafes to those who only for a time have been led astray by passion. Being given over to his new guide in the Earthly Paradise on the top of the Purgatorial Mount, and having seen there in a vision the symbolic history of the Church and her degeneration up to his own time, and having received from Beatrice the comforting assurance that a lawgiver or Saviour would shortly appear, he mounts up with his friend by sheer force of inspired longing toward heaven, traverses the heavenly Paradise from planet to planet, through the fixed stars and the heavenly spheres, and sees there the glorification of all the souls which in their earthly life furthered the great work of the education of humanity in its double aspect of temporal and spiritual happiness: wise lawgivers and great emperors, the saintly theologians and Fathers of the Church, martyrs and defenders of the faith, as well as all great statesmen. At last, in the highest heaven, he beholds the whole company of the redeemed ranged round the Trinity, and shows in inspired dreams the ideal of spiritual and temporal order, which he would so gladly have seen realized upon earth, and to which all his life he had devoted the best powers of head and heart.[1]

Not a little significant is the fact that this burning spiritual song was given to the world under the modest title of *The Comedy*, in the original

---

[1] *Vide* Weber: *Weltgeschichte*, p. 801.

sense of a song of joy (κῶμος and ᾠδή); for, though it begins in sadness, it ends with the highest joy, and that it was the heart of the people that found it to be *divine*. When the title *Divina Commedia* was first used is not quite certain. It occurs in the Venice edition of 1516, and in the frontispiece to that of Giolito dei Ferrari of 1554. Dante makes a broad distinction between the *tragic*, the *comic*, and the *elegiac* style. The tragic style, which is that of Homer and Virgil, he calls sublime, and speaks of the "high tragedy" of the Æneid. That of comedy, on the other hand, is the "inferior" or "middle" style; whilst the "elegiac" is that in which the sorrowful can best express themselves. In thus modestly styling his poem

Commedia our author would have us understand a "narration" or "representation," simple, calm, and clear, in the homely speech of the people. Instead of singing his great thoughts in Latin, which was the language of his master, Virgil, and indeed that of the cultured classes generally, the poet-exile was content with Italian, and so has for ever spoken to the heart of the nation. And the form of the poem, the simple *terza rima*, greatly adds to the purity and depth of the ideas. The whole structure consists of some fifteen thousand lines in tierce rhyme, consisting of tercets in which the last word of the middle line of each gives the rhyme to the first and third lines of the following tercet, so that all the tercets of each canto continue the action by interpenetration. But, as the first tercet starts the rhymes by its middle line, it follows that the first and third lines of the first tercet stand out by themselves as a pair of rhymed lines, and at the end of each canto there is a similar pair.

Prof. Tomlinson represents the structure geometrically, thus :—

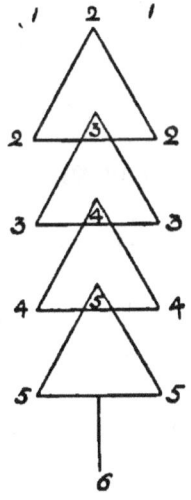

The poem is divided into three great parts: Hell, Purgatory, and Paradise. According to the Ptolemaic system which prevailed at that time, the earth was considered to be the fixed centre of creation, and the sun a planet revolving round her, which, together with the other planets, was "under the immediate guidance of angels, archangels, thrones, principalities, and powers." The earth and heavens were thus interdependent, and between them were the spheres of air and of fire. From the latter proceeded meteors, lightning, and the aurora, and beyond this sphere of fire was what was known as the heaven of the moon, inhabited by those who had broken the vow of chastity. Mars was the abode of Christian warriors; Venus of lovers; Jupiter of righteous rulers; Mercury contained the souls of patriot kings and active spirits, whilst Saturn was the seat of contemplative saints. The host of the triumph of Christ was to be found in the heaven of the fixed stars; the Empyrean was the sphere of God's visible presence, and the Primum Mobile the sphere of the divine glory.

Now, when Satan was hurled "headlong, flaming, from the ethereal sky," he is said to have fallen about where Jerusalem now stands, and that, shrinking from the polluting contact, this part of the earth's surface at once formed itself into a great conical cavity, a gigantic amphitheatre, with manifold gradations and diminishingly small arena—Hell, the everlasting dwelling-place of the unrepentant, the centre of the earth and the centre of gravity, presided over by the Prince of the powers of darkness. Exactly opposite Hell, about where the most southern Society Islands lie, there was formed, by the portion of earth thus displaced, a great and high mountain, rising out of the wilderness of waters, Purgatory, the Mount of Purification. As a result of this terrific convulsion the Earthly Paradise was removed to the summit of this mountain, where the law of gravitation was no longer in force, and whence the purified soul, unfettered, would wing its way to Heaven.

On Good Friday of the year 1300, when he had reached the middle age of thirty-five, and that period of life when, as Dante tells us in one of his earlier works, reason triumphs over the passions, the poet's vision begins.

He finds himself in a darksome lonely wood, having lost the beaten path.

> Ahi quanto a dir qual era è cosa dura
> Questa selva selvaggia e aspra e forte,
> Che nel pensier rinnova la paura!
> Tanto è amara, che poco è più morte.

> "*Ah me! how hard it were to make it clear,*
> *What was this strong, rough forest, tangled o'er,*
> *Which only in the thought renews the fear,*
> *So bitter 'tis, e'en Death is little more.*"

The forest is symbolical not only of the vices of the age and of the moral and political chaos of Italy, but generally of the sins of youth. Whilst struggling on, he sees in the distance the delectable mountain, the top of which is illumined by the Sun of righteousness. At this glad sight he takes courage, and loses no time in pressing forward to climb this hill of happiness; but hardly is he out of the wood when three wild beasts rush at him and drive him out of the path. That the panther, the lion, and the she-wolf are symbolical of sinful passions there can be no doubt; *what* these sins are is, after all, a matter of minor importance. They are generally supposed to be Sensuality, Pride, and Avarice, the characteristic passions of youth, of manhood, and of old age. Such fear do these three beasts work in him that he flees, and is well-nigh giving up all hope of the hill of divine peace, when suddenly he becomes aware of the presence of one

> Chi per lungo silenzio parea fioco;

"Who hoarse appeared through silence long sustained";

and, lo! it was the Bard of Mantua. On seeing Virgil, Dante exclaims :—

> O degli altri poeti onore e lume,
>   Vagliami il lungo studio e il grande amore
>   Che m'han fatto cercar lo tuo volume.
> Tu se' lo mio maestro e il mio autore :
>   Tu se' solo colui, da cui io tolsi
>   Lo bello stile, che m'ha fatto onore.

> "O light and pride of all the bards that sing!
>   May the great love, long study profit me,
>   Which to explore thy volume me did bring.
> In thee my Master, Author, too, I see,
>   For thou art he alone, from whom I won
>   The beauteous style that made me honoured be."

Here, then, was Lo buon Maestro,

famoso Saggio, Caro Duca mio, as Dante calls Virgil, one who could help him to overcome the beasts. But Virgil at once tells Dante that he will not forthwith succeed in curbing these passions. He must first be led to a sense of the awfulness of sin by going down into Hell, and after that he must visit Purgatory to know the blessedness of repentance, before he will be fit for a vision of Heaven. Through Hell and Purgatory, Virgil will conduct him, but for the celestial regions

>Anima fia a ciò di me più degna;
>Con lei ti lascerò nel mio partire :

"*A soul shall come, worthier for that than I;
I'll place thee 'neath her guidance, quitting mine.*"

Now, upon a right understanding of the character and function of Dante's second guide really depends the meaning of the whole work. For the weird and gloomy circles of Hell and for the steep ascent of Purgatory there could be no more fitting guide than Virgil, the singer of Æneas' descent into Hell. To the middle age Virgil was amongst poets what Aristotle was amongst philosophers, and the forms of heathen mythology were not looked upon as figures bodied forth arbitrarily, but rather as perverted truth which had a meaning even for Christendom. Thus, in Christian Dante's under-world we find heathen gods and demi-gods as demons, and our poet does not hesitate to invoke the aid of Apollo and the

Muses. But when we come to the Paradiso, it is Beatrice, the glorified.

> "The woman-soul leadeth us
> Upward and on."

It is true she does not actually appear until the end of the Purgatorio, but it is most important that we should notice well the way she is introduced in the second canto of the *Inferno*. Here Dante's courage fails. He says to Virgil:—

> Ma io perchè venirvi? o chi 'l concede?
> Io non Enea, io non Paolo sono ·
> Me degno a ciò nè io nè altri crede.

> " *Why should I go? from whom concession gain?*
> *I'm not Æneas, and not Paul am I:*
> *Nor I, nor others, worthy would me deign.*"

To this Virgil answers, that, if he has rightly understood him, his soul is infected with cowardice, which is the root of failure in every noble enterprise. He then goes on to explain in what way he was led to come to Dante's rescue. Whilst in Limbo, of which Dante says in the fourth canto :—

> Quivi, secondo che per ascoltare,
>   Non avea pianto, ma che di sospiri,
>   Che l'aura eterna facevan tremare :
> E ciò avvenia di duol senza martiri,
>   Ch'avean le turbe, ch' eran molti e grandi,
>   E d'infanti e di femmine e di viri.

" *Here as by listening I became aware,*
  There was no lamentation, save of sighs,
  Which caused a trembling in the eternal air:
From sorrow without pangs did this arise
  From out the crowds which numerous were
       and great,
  Of infants, women, and of men likewise."

Virgil says :—

Io era tra color che son sospesi
    E Donna mi chiamò beata e bella,
    Tal che di comandare io la richiesi.
Lucevan gli occhi suoi più che la Stella
    E cominciommi a dir soave e piana,
    Con angelica voce, in sua favella :
O anima cortese Mantovana,
    Di cui la fama ancor nel mondo dura,
    E durerà quanto il mondo lontana,
L'amico mio, e non della ventura,
    Nella diserta piaggia è impedito
    Sì nel cammin, che volto è per paura :
E temo che non sia già sì smarrito,
    Ch' io mi sia tardi al soccorso levata,
    Per quel ch' i' ho di lui nel Cielo udito.
Or muovi, e con la tua parola ornata
    E con ciò c' ha mestieri al suo campare,
    L'aiuta sì ch'io ne sia consolata.
I' son Beatrice, che ti faccio andare :

" A saintly Lady called me, one so fair,
    I begged her to command my service free.
Her eyes shone brighter than the star ; and clear
    And soft her angel voice, when she began
    In her own tongue thus to address mine ear:

O courteous spirit of the Mantuan!
   Whose fame yet in the world hath known no
     . *end,*
   Fame that will last as long as motion can ;

A friend of mine, of Fortune not a friend,
   Now on the desert slope upon his way
   Is hindered, and through dread would back-
      ward wend :
He may, I fear, be so much gone astray,
   That I have risen to his aid too late,
   From that which I of him in Heaven heard
      say.
Now hasten thou, and with thy speech ornate,
   And with what else it needs for his release,
   Assist him, so that I be consolate ;
I who now bid thee go am Beatrice.' "

Most willingly does Virgil undertake to do this, at the same time expressing his surprise that Beatrice should come to such a place as Limbo to find him. Then she unfolds to him how in Heaven "a gentle Lady," symbolical of divine Mercy, called her to the mission.

> Donna è gentil nel Ciel, che si Compiange
>   Di questo impedimento, ov' io ti mando,
>   Si che duro giudicio lassù frange.
> Questa chiese Lucia in suo dimando,
>   E disse: Ora abbisogna il tuo fedele
>   Di te, ed io a te lo raccomando.
> Lucia nimica di ciascun crudele
>   Si mosse, e venne al loco dov' io era,
>   Che mi sedea con l'antica Rachele.
> Disse: Beatrice, loda di Dio vera,
>   Che non soccorri quei che t' amò tanto,
>   Ch' uscio per te della volgare schiera?
> Non odi tu la pièta del suo pianto?
>   Non vedi tu la morte che 'l combatte
>   Su la fiumana, onde il mar non ha vanto?

> " *A gentle Lady doth in Heaven complain*
>   *Of this impediment, to which thou'rt sent;*
>   *So there stern judgment broken doth remain.*
> *With her request to Lucia she went*
>   *And said: 'Thy faithful one needs aid from*
>   *thee.*

I recommend him unto thy intent.'
Lucia, the foe of every cruelty,
    Bestirred herself, and came to the place where I
    With ancient Rachel sat in company.

And said: ' True praise of God, O Beatrice, why
    Dost thou not succour him who loved thee so,
    That he, for thee, the vulgar herd did fly?
Dost thou not hear his piteous cries of woe?
    Nor see death combat him that flood beside,
    O'er which the ocean can no boasting know?'"

The four ladies here mentioned are at once real and symbolical. The "gentle Lady" is the Virgin, who represents the Mercy of God; Lucia is the martyr of Syracuse, symbolizing radiating Grace; Rachel is at once the wife of the patriarch and the Contemplative Life; whilst Beatrice is both the poet's early

Love and Heavenly Wisdom or the knowledge of God.

Arrived at the vestibule of Hell, the poets behold over its gloomy portals the awful inscription :—

> Lasciate ogni speranza, voi che entrate.
> "*Abandon hope, all ye who enter here!*"

Here they meet with those sad souls who are "without praise and without shame," who are neither faithful to God nor man, but just live for themselves. Hafis truly says, "Any Kibla that may be is better than self-worship"; and certainly this was Dante's view, for, never were more trenchant words spoken of any one than those he puts into the mouth of Virgil on this occasion :—

> Non ragioniam di lor, ma guarda e passa.
> "*Speak we not of them: only look and pass!*"

Passing over the first circle with the spirits of the unbaptized poets and philosophers, we come to those who are eternally agitated by the most cruel winds in foulest atmosphere. And here we have one of Dante's tenderest touches, which show us how deep a heart lay within that lofty frame. Amongst the luxurious and the lustful our poet recognises Francesca da Rimini, and hears her pathetic story :—

> Amor, che al cor gentil ratto s'apprende,
>   Prese costui della bella persona
>   Che mi fu tolta, e 'l modo ancor m'offende.
> Amor, ch'a nullo amato amar perdona,
>   Mi prese del costui piacer sì forte,
>   Che, com vedi, ancor non m'abbandona.
> Amor condusse noi ad una morte :
>   Caina attende chi in vita ci spense.
>   Queste parole da lor ci fur porte.

Da che io intesi quelle anime offense,
   Chinai il viso, e tanto il tenni basso,
   Finchè 'l Poeta mi disse: Che pense?
Quando riposi, cominciai: O lasso,
   Quanti dolci pensier, quanto disio
   Menò costoro al doloroso passo!
Poi mi rivolsi a loro, e parla' io;
   E cominciai: Francesca, i tuoi martiri
   A lagrimar mi fanno tristo e pio.
Ma dimmi: al tempo de' dolci sospiri,
   A che e come concedette Amore,
   Che conosceste i dubbiosi desiri?
Ed ella a me: Nessun maggior dolore,
   Che ricordarsi del tempo felice
   Nella miseria; e ciò sa 'l tuo Dottore.
Ma se a conoscer la prima radice
   Del nostro amor tu hai cotanto affetto,
   Farò come colui che piange e dice.
Noi leggevamo un giorno, per diletto,
   Di Lancilotto, come amor lo strinse:
   Soli eravamo e senz' alcun sospetto.
Per più fiate gli occhi ci sospinse
   Quella lettura, e scolorocci il viso:
   Ma solo un punto fu quel che ci vinse.

Quando leggemmo il disiato riso
    Esser baciato da cotanto amante,
    Questi, che mai da me non fia diviso,

La bocca mi baciò tutto tremante:
    Galeotto fu 'l libro e chi lo scrisse :
    Quel giorno più non vi leggemmo avante.

Mentre che l'uno spirto questo disse,
    L'altro piangeva sì, che di pietade
    I'venni men così com' io morisse ;
E caddi, come corpo morto cade.

" ' *Love, that on gentle heart swiftly attends,*
    Seized him by reason of the person fair
    *Ta'en from me in a mode that still
    offends.*

Love that lets no beloved 'scape loving care,
    Seized me ; so strong my love of him became
    That as thou seest, it quitteth me not here.

Love brought us unto death, one and the same ;
    Caina waits for him, who took our life.'
    *Such were the words from them to us that
    came.*

*When I had heard those souls oppressed with
   grief,
I bent my head, so long held down my face,
Till 'What dost think?' was the Poet's
   question brief.
When I replied, I thus began : ' Alas!
How many dulcet thoughts, how much
   desire
Conducted them unto the dolorous pass!'
Then unto them I turned me to inquire,
And spake : 'Francesca, all thine agonies
Make me to weep sad tears, and ruth in-
   spire.
But tell me : at the time of the sweet sighs,
By what, and in what way, did love con-
   cede
That dubious longings you should recog-
   nise?'
And she to me, 'No greater grief we heed,
Than to be minded of the happy time
In misery ; and such thy Teacher's creed.
But if to know our love's root in its prime
The wish so strong a hold on thee doth take,
Like one who weeps and speaks, I'll do
   like him.*

> We read one day, for delectation's sake
> Of Lancelot, how love did him compel:
> Alone were we; nought made suspicion
>   wake.
> Full many a time that reading did impel
> Our eyes to meet, and paled each face the
>   while:
> What conquered us, one point alone can
>   tell.
> When we were reading of the longed-for smile
> Which such a noble lover kissed of yore,
> This one, who ne'er from me is separable,
> Kissed me upon the mouth, trembling all o'er:
> Galeotto was the book, and he who writ:
> That day we read within that book no
>   more.'
> And all the while one spirit uttered it,
> The other wept, and pity did so plead,
> I fainted quite, as in a dying fit,
> And fell, as falls a body that is dead!"

In the twenty-eighth canto Dante depicts the sufferings of those who brought about discord in the community and schism in religion. The sin of schism was one which our poet's soul abhorred: hence the awful picture here drawn of the spirits that live in perpetual self-laceration. Amongst these are Muhammad˘and Ali, who face each other and tear their flesh, representing the attitude of the Sunnis and Shias.

> Vedi come storpiato è Maometto:
>   Dinanzi a me sen va piangendo Ali,
>   Fesso nel volto dal mento al ciuffetto:
> E tutti gli altri, che tu vedi qui,
>   Seminator di scandalo e di scisma
>   Fur vivi, e però son fessi così.

The horrible sights and sounds of the ninth and tenth *bolgie* so affect the Pilgrim that he speaks of his eyes as being drunken with wounds, and of language as failing him to describe the tortures resulting from those sins which are punished by *la ministra dell' alto Sire, infallibil giustizia,* "Righteousness infallible, servant of the Most High."

On entering Giudecca, Dante follows Virgil, who shows him Lucifer, formerly "the most beautiful of all God's creatures," now the most abandoned of the fallen. Having reached his middle they have found the centre of the earth, and thenceforth mount "to see again the stars."

In passing on to the *Purgatorio*, we see for the first time the Star of Hope gleaming on the trembling waters.

"Watching, with eternal lids apart,
 Like Nature's patient, sleepless Eremite,
 The moving waters at their priest-like task
 Of pure ablution round earth's human shores."

Gross darkness is left behind, the dew

is on the lotus, a rainbow smiles upon the shining sea, that bridge divine from Mannaheim to Asaheim, from the home of man to the Home of God, as we have it in the bold and beautiful Saga of the North. What a beautiful thought! Early on Easter morning the pilgrim of the Inferno, having girded himself with a reed, symbolic of the Washing of Repentance, issues forth with his guide on to the Mount of Purification. "Repentance," says a Chinese proverb, "is the May of virtues." "That trembling of the ocean-waves (tremolar dell' onde)," as Carlyle says, "under the first pure gleam of morning, dawning afar on the wandering Two, is as the type of an altered mood. Hope has now dawned; never-dying Hope, if in company still with heavy sorrow. The obscure sojourn of dæmons and reprobate is underfoot; a soft breathing of penitence mounts higher and higher, to the Throne of Mercy itself. 'Pray for me,' the denizens of that Mount of Pain all say to him. 'Tell my Giovanna to pray for me, my daughter Giovanna; I think her mother loves me no more!' They toil painfully up that winding steep, 'bent down like corbels of a building,' some of them—crushed together so 'for the sin of pride'; yet nevertheless in years, in ages and æons, they shall have reached the top, which is Heaven's gate, and by Mercy shall have been admitted in. The joy too of all, when one has prevailed; the whole mountain shakes with joy, and a psalm of praise rises when one soul has perfected repentance, and got its sin and misery left behind. I call this the noble embodiment of a true, noble thought."

Unlike the condemned spirits of the Inferno, those in Purgatory rejoice in their sufferings. All punishment is purification. Amongst the gluttons Dante recognises Forese de' Donati, who explains:—

> E non pur una volta, questo spazzo
>   Girando, si rinfresca nostra pena:
>   Io dico pena, e dovre' dir sollazzo;
> Chè quella voglia all' arbore ci mena,
> Che menò Cristo lieto a dire Elì
> Quando ne liberò con la sua vena.

The *Purgatorio* gives us so much of Dante's psychology that we shall do well to look at it in that light.

The *soul* is throughout one and individual; the rational, God-given soul draws the nature-given faculties (the sensitive and the vegetative) into its own circle, and makes them one with itself. To the Platonic view, which ascribes several souls to man, Dante makes the empirical objection, that if a pleasant or painful sensation, or indeed any engrossing perception, takes possession of consciousness, all other presentative faculties are cut off (*Purg.* iv. 1). But this does not prevent one's holding distinct powers of the soul and their complete substantiation: memory, for instance, incites phantasy to recall the past. When, however, one of the soul's faculties is engaged, when there is a strong sense-impression, the other senses seem extinguished,[1] and even Imagination may so take possession of us that we become oblivious of trumpet-blasts around us;[2] in this case the soul is no longer itself, self-consciousness leaves it:—

Un' alma sola, che vive e sente e sè in sè rigira.[3]

The opposite state is when it is *intera*. Hence for Dante, to whom the oneness of personality is of such great importance, the *intero* assumes a moral aspect: it is that which is true to itself and becomes corrupt by nothing outside:—

Mardocheo, che fu al dire ed al far così 'ntero.[4]

Whoever is not capable of this concentration, in whom various thoughts

[1] *Purg.* xxxii. 1.   [2] *Purg.* xvii. 13.
[3] *Purg.* xxv. 74.   [4] *Purg.* xvii. 29.

are constantly succeeding one another, will arrive at no goal, because the energy of the one nullifies that of the other. And as for the individual so also for the race, the highest goal is to reach Unity; for we must strive after likeness to God, who is wholly One and individual.

Nevertheless this concentration need not be absolutely internal, but, as we have seen, may affect an external object; when, for instance, music is heard, the soul is *intera*, because then the life-spirits are almost all brought into action, *e la virtù di' tutti quasi corre allo spirito sensibile che riceve il suono;* similarly a wish may get so ardent that one becomes well-nigh incapable of speaking of anything else.

The immortality of the soul is to Dante a self-evident dogma, which needs neither explanation nor justification. In the *Inferno* we read : "On this side are the graves of Epicurus and all his followers, who say that the soul dies with the body." To the heretics belongs also that Cardinal who had said as he was dying, "If there is a soul, then I have lost it for the Ghibellines." The soul being an immediate gift of God, it must be a sin against Him to doubt its imperishability or even its existence. To deny this Immortality is indeed stupidity, a contradiction; for, inasmuch as many have already renounced the present life for the sake of that which is beyond, Man, instead of being the most perfect creature—which indeed he is—

would be the most imperfect. But, he adds, as to whether the immortal part in us is corporeal or incorporeal, opinions differ. To change this sorrow-laden earthly life for the heavenly was Dante's heart's desire; it need therefore be no surprise to find him eagerly defending Immortality.

The relationship of *body* and *soul* is to him a purely dualistic one, although, in a theologico-metaphysical sense, the mind is the final cause of the physical. When the formation of the fœtus is sufficiently advanced for it to be able to move and have sensation as an animal, God, delighted with Nature's art-work, comes to him, and breathes into him a *new* mind, the higher soul-faculty, whilst the material part is formed from materials which were already there, and at death becomes absolutely separated from the spiritual element. Thus the dead soul forms for itself a shadow-body from the air by which it is surrounded. In that lovely and touching scene in the *Purgatorio* (xxi. 130) between Statius and Virgil, when the former learns that Virgil is before him, he bends at once to kiss his feet, but Virgil holds him back with, "We are both but shadows"; and he, "Now thou canst measure the greatness of my consuming love for thee, which led me to forget that we are shadows, and to clasp shadows as though they were solid bodies." In spite of this altogether different origin, end, and essence, the soul is most intimately connected with the body, gathering up into a relatively unified whole the elements presented to it, as in wine the sun's heat unites with the sap in the vine, it resolves itself into different members having different functions, as God shows Himself in manifold fulfilment in the stars.[1]

Amongst the imperfections of life Dante feels most keenly the incapacity of Language to adequately express thoughts and feelings. Once he says: "Had I but the fulness of power to express it, which I have to think it out!" Our mind is better able to think than to speak. In a dedication to Can Grande he says: "Multa namque per intellectum videmus, quibus signa vocalia desunt." Language must, of course, share the

[1] *Par.* ii. 133.

common human imperfection, for it serves to show us that of which we are still in ignorance, and the state of Ignorance is characteristic of mortals as opposed to the heavenly beings, who have absolute knowledge in the contemplation of God. Hence the angels have no language, as they have nothing more to communicate. Nevertheless, he is not insensible to the incomparable importance of Language to us; not only because it has come to us straight from God, but inasmuch as it is as necessary an instrument for our ideas as the horse is to the soldier; and as the best soldier uses the best horse, so the best idea the most complete speech. Nay, it is successful in effecting what is, after all, the most powerful and wonderful, namely, in moving the human heart; hence Dante interprets the Orpheus-saga allegorically, in the sense of the wise man who *with his voice* understands how to tame and lead cruel and rough hearts, which are like stones and wild beasts. Thus his pessimism concerning Language is not thoroughgoing; he recognises that words adjust themselves to subjects, that in them primitive wisdom is hidden, nay, so great is the power of the sweetness of the simple word Amor, that he cannot imagine that anything Amor does can be other than sweet. In one point, however, he makes a difference between things and their linguistic expression, namely, that a correct conclusion can be drawn from false premises; for, inasmuch as the True in itself can never follow from the false, it is only the *signs* of the True which can come from the *signs* for the false.

It was only natural that a poet who was to creatively mould his language to purposes quite new, and thus to form a new language, should be deeply sensible alike of the power and the limitation of linguistic expression; indeed, it is of such value to him that, in his opinion, a translated poetic work would be without beauty and harmony. Very significant is the fact that the laudatory passages on language occur in his early writings, whilst those of complaint are to be found in the *Commedia*. Here, too, prose is said to have greater power of expression than poetry, whereas formerly he had sought the model which prose-writers should always follow in the poets. In fact, the linguistic question is to Dante a branch of that dualism of which to him the world consists: since men differ from each other infinitely, they need means of communication — mere movements or gesticulation, such as the animals make use of, would not be sufficiently intelligible, nor would the purely spiritual intercommunication of the angels do; hence the vehicle of thought must be at once rational and sensual: and this is just what language is; as sound sensuous, as full of meaning rational and conceptual.

But that human incapacity to be equal in language to an overwhelmingly

momentous question or subject, is carried up even into the faculty of thought itself: "That which I must now describe a voice has never expressed, a pen described, nor even phantasy ever conceived." Dante calls the Muses to his aid, having things to sing which even to think are difficult. Hence the inability of our intellect to arrive at things to which phantasy cannot help us.

Perhaps the continual change to which languages are subject is the cause of their imperfection. As an instance, our poet gives the variety of names for il sommo Bene, namely, God.[1]

[1] In the twenty-sixth canto of the *Paradiso* (130) our poet puts into Adam's mouth the following remarkable words:—

By mutual arrangement, therefore, the immutable Latin was adopted, the dialects retaining the difference, and only the Language of the Heart being the same for all. The infinite variety, the constant change, which is everywhere inseparable from humanity, is the more intimately bound up with the linguistic question, as Dante obviously accepts a fundamental connexion between language and people; he classi-

>Opera naturale è ch' uom favella
>>Ma, così o così, natura lascia
>>Poi fare a voi secondo che v'abbella.
>Pria ch' io scendesi all' infernale ambascia,
>>*I* s' appellava in terra il sommo Bene
>>Onde vien la letizia che mi fascia;
>*Eli* si chiamò poi: e ciò conviene;
>>Chè l' uso de' mortali è come fronda
>>In ramo, che sen va, ed altra viene.

F

fies nations according to the word they have for Yes, and characterizes Italy as the land dove 'l si si parla.[1]

On quitting Purgatory, Dante is taken up by Beatrice into the Empyrean, where the moving principle of the heavenly spheres is the longing after God. Here he beholds that great company which no man can number, out of every nation, kindred, tribe, and tongue, those who have come out of great tribulation, have washed their robes, and now, in white stoles, stand before the throne of the Divine! Our poet feels himself a child and appeals to his celestial guide. She unfolds to him the

[1] See a most interesting article in the *Zeitschrift für Sprachwissenschaft und Völkerpsychologie*, by Georg Simmel: Dante's Psychologie.

nature of the world, the origin of evil, and the secret of Redemption. He breathes "an ampler ether, a diviner air," as he becomes aware how, led by the pilot Love, souls set sail for different havens in the great Sea of Being.

Amor is the beginning, middle, end of Paradise; Amor which moves the sun and all the stars. With St. Paul the poet says: "Though I speak with the tongues of men and of angels, and have not love, I have become as sounding brass or a tinkling cymbal."

Looking upon Dante with the compassion of a mother for her delirious child, Beatrice says:—

>   . . . Le cose tutte quante
> Hann' ordine tra loro ; e questo è forma
> Che l'universo a Dio fa simigliante.

What is this *ordine*, the *Ṛta* of the Vêdic poets, the *Aṡa* of the " wise men from the East " ?—It is Love, whereby the universe becomes an image of the divine Principle, which turns Chaos into Kosmos, and forms the world into a well-ordered and beautiful structure. Nay, when in the *Purgatorio* he explains how he came to be the author of those matchless lines :

> Donne, ch' avete intelletto d' amore,

our poet ascribes all his eminence in verse to the same noble influence, to a lofty love which takes possession of the soul.

And now Dante is realizing and enjoying to the full the New Life of which he wrote in early youth. In

Paradise he sees not only women, but men " with the intellect of love." And this life of love leads him to a very significant view of truth. According to Dante it is possible for us all to know truth, and from a knowledge of particular truths, purified and strengthened by previous Doubt, to arrive at the highest Truth, namely, knowledge of God.

Io veggio ben che giammai non si sazia
    Nostro intelleto, se il Ver non lo illustra,
    Di fuor dal qual nessun vero si spazia.

Posasi in esso come fera in lustra,
    Tosto che giunto l' ha: e giugner puollo;
    Se non, ciascun disio sarebbe frustra.

Nasce per quello, a guisa di rampollo,
    Appiè del vero il dubbio: ed è natura,
    Ch' al sommo pinge noi di collo in collo.

Full well I see at peace is ne'er our mind
  Unless the Light of Truth upon it fall,
  Outside of which we nothing true can find.

And as the lion in his lair doth rest,
  So rests a human soul in Truth, when found;
  And found it can be, else were vain all quest.

And pure desire.   As, too, upon the tree,
  The shoot, so groweth Doubt at foot of Truth
  And leads from height to height to make us free!
              —*Par.* iv. 124.

The Peace of Paradise is in the Will of God, toward which the whole creation moves :—

> In la sua volontade è nostra pace :
>   Ella è quel mare al qual tutto si muove
>   Ciò ch' ella cria e che natura face.

In the *Paradiso* it is only natural that we should find our poet's theology, and it is worthy of note that Dante shows a marvellous depth and breadth in this respect. As regards the anthropomorphism of the old Testament, for instance, he says:—

> Per questo la Scrittura condescende
> A vostra facultate, e piedi e mano
> Attribuisce a Dio, ed altro intende.

Respecting the composition of the *Paradiso* there is a curious story related by Boccaccio on the authority of Petro Giardino of Ravenna. Whilst writing it, it was Dante's custom to send a few cantos at a time to Messer Can Grande della Scala, who, after reading them, ordered copies to be made. "In this way all but the last thirteen cantos reached Messer Cane, when the poet died without having mentioned them to any one. Dante's sons searched diligently for them, but could not find them; whereupon several of their friends requested them to finish the poem. They had actually commenced their presumptuous task when a vision appeared to Jacopo, who was the more ardent of the two in the matter, which revealed to him where the missing cantos were to be found. In the ninth month after the poet's decease, one night near the hour of matins, Jacopo went to the house of one Petro Giardino, of Ravenna, an earnest disciple of Dante, and told him that in his sleep he had just seen a figure of his father clad in white raiment, and his face shining with a supernatural light; and that, on his asking if he were still alive, he replied, 'Yes, but with the true life, not with the life of this world.' Whereupon he asked him if he had finished his work before he departed to the true life; and if he had, what he had done with the concluding cantos, since they could nowhere be found. 'Yes, I finished it,' answered the luminous figure, and forthwith taking the hand of his son led him to the chamber where he had been accustomed to sleep, and, touching a part of the wall, said: 'Here is that which you have so long sought for.' And these words having been spoken, the dream came to an end. Jacopo was so affected that he immediately rose and sought out his friend Petro Giardino, to tell him of his dream, and request him to accompany him in the place indicated. So they went together, it still being dark, to the house where Dante died, and calling up the master they proceeded to the place pointed out. There was a piece of matting fastened against the wall, as they had before noticed when Dante lived there. On removing it an opening was discovered behind, and in it they found many writings which had become mouldy from the damp, and would have perished had they remained there much longer. Having carefully cleaned them, they perceived the numbers of the missing cantos, and found to their joy that the papers contained the conclusion of the poem—the last thirteen. These they gladly copied, and sent them to Messer Cane, and thus the labour of so many years was rendered perfect."

Now, in order to fully understand the central figure of the Poem, we must bear in mind that the *Divine Comedy* is part of a Trilogy consisting of *Vita Nuova*, *Amoroso Convivio*, and *Divina Commedia*.

When still a child, Dante's innocent heart was aflame with love for Beatrice, daughter of Folco Portinari. The attachment, which was mutual, began when they were both about nine years old, and lasted, in Dante's case, even after Beatrice had become the wife of Simone dei Bardi. The *Vita Nuova*, which was probably written in 1292, after Beatrice's death, is the book of this pure and lofty love, this childlike living piety, beholding everywhere the finger of God and the riches of His grace.

Questa gentilissima, la quale fù distruggitrice di tutti li vizj, e reina delle virtù.

When Beatrice approaches a

Spirito d' Amore, distruggendo tutti gli altri spiriti sensitivi,

drives out the Spiriti del viso, and takes their place.

"I say that when she appeared in any place the hope of her adorable salutation worked upon me in such a way that I seemed no longer to have an enemy, and such a glow of charity came over me that I could have forgiven any one who had offended me; and if any one had asked anything of me, my only reply would have been, 'Love!' with humility depicted on my face. . . . And when this most gentle lady saluted, love, so far from being the means of overshadowing my intolerable beatitude, produced in me such sovereign sweetness that my body, being wholly subject thereto, often became as it were an inanimate mass. Hence it was manifest that my beatitude was in her salutation, although it produced effects on me beyond my powers of endurance."

"This most gentle lady rose so much in favour with all men, that as she went along people ran to look at her; which rejoiced me greatly. And when she was near any one, so much truth entered his heart, that he dared not raise his eyes on her or return her salutation, as many can testify from experience. She went on her way crowned and clothed with humility, and displayed no pride at what she saw and heard. And when she had passed by, many said: 'That is not a woman, but one of the most beautiful angels of heaven!' And others said: 'This is a marvel! Blessed be the Lord who can work so admirably!' I say that she was so gentle and replete with every pleasant gift and grace, that those who looked on her experienced a sweet and tender feeling which cannot be described. And no one could look on her without sighing. These, and still more wonderful things, were produced by her marvellous virtue. Hence, thinking on these things, and wishing to devote something to her praise to embalm, as it were, her excellent and marvellous power, not only for the sake of those who had known her, but, so far as words could do it, to convey some idea of her to those who knew her not, to this end I wrote the following sonnet :—

" When she, my lady, greets folk with ' Good-day,'
    Such candour and such gentleness combine,
    That tongues grow tremulous and speech resign,
And to look on her no one dare essay.
She feels men's praises as she goes her way
    In meekness clad, an influence benign;
    You fancy she must be a thing divine,
Come down from heaven, a marvel to display.
Her presence is so pleasant to the eye,
    That through the eye the heart with sweetness glows:
To understand it, you its power must prove.
And from those lips an influence seems to move
    So sweet and full of love, it overflows,
And goes on saying to our spirit : ' Sigh ! ' " [1]

---

[1] See *The Sonnet, its Origin,* etc., by C. Tomlinson, F.R.S.

When, however, he arrives at full manhood, to his intense grief, the object of his affection is taken from him. He mourns as for lost innocence. But at length a new charm entices him. In the looks of a fair maiden he thinks he can recover the love and mercy of Beatrice. "When," he says, "this lady looked at me, it was with a face so pious and pallid, as though it were of love, that I was often reminded of my most noble lady." She promises to comfort and console, and indeed it is not long before her flashing eyes repress the memory of the dear departed and take full possession of his heart. This second lady is none other than the queen of that vasty, speculative deep, which is lighted mostly by the moon. To this painful and

baneful second love, Philosophy, the
Amoroso Convivio is dedicated. It is a
restless and calamitous affection, for the
peace of childlike devotion has vanished
from his breast. He is ever asking
some new favour of the Beloved; sometimes she turns herself away from him,
and then loud are his sighs and moans;
at times, too, he feels that this love can
never bring lasting satisfaction to his
heart.

She leads him to philosophize upon
everything which comes before him.
He investigates the nature of righteousness, of valour, and of nobility; he
develops his principles of statesmanship;
he weighs well the great events of his
time, and dedicates his life to what he
considers true. Now it is that he is

drawn into the vortex of party politics, which oblige him to take so leading a part in his native city. This also is the time when he develops his views on *language* and *poetry*. So keen is the conflict of opinion, the noise of many waters, the glare of many lights, that he thenceforth resolves to leave the allurements of the world and to tread the steep and lonely paths of Speculation in order to be able to look into the sunlight of Eternal Truth and to know the nature of God. Here however he has soon to learn how mistaken is the way he has chosen, how insufficient all earthly Reason is where only Revelation can lead to the goal. In one of his *canzone* our poet says:—

Le dolci rime d' amor ch' io solia
Cercar ne' miei pensieri,
Convien ch' io lasci, non perch' io non speri
Ad esse ritornare;
Ma perchè gli atti disdegnosi e feri
Che nella donna mia
Sono appariti, in' han chiuso la via
Dell' usato parlare.

Again, in the *Vita Nuova* we read :—

Allora lo mio cuore incominciò dolorosamente a pentirsi del desidero, a cui così vilmente s' avea lasciato possedere alquanti di contro alla costanza della ragione, e discacciato questo cotal malvagio desiderio, si rivolsero tutti i miei pensamenti alla loro gentilissima Beatrice.

"Man täuscht sich," says Witte, "wenn man, wie geschehen ist, diesen, von Dante auf das unzweideutigste ausgesprochenen, Gegensatz von Religion und Philosophie für eine Besonderheit *unserer* Zeit hält. Nicht nur dass er in allen Zeitaltern wiederkehrt, so trat er gerade im späteren Mittelalter mit besonderer Entschiedenheit hervor. Allerdings redete die Philosophie jener Tage durchgängig eine christliche Sprache ; aber

durch ihr Bestreben, die Wahrheit, wenn auch in
Uebereinstimmung mit dem Glauben, doch auf
selbstständigem Wege zu finden, trat sie in ausgesprochenen Gegensatz zur Kirche. Ohne an
die Kämpfe Abälard's und seiner Nachfolger zu
erinnern, war das dreizehnte Jahrhundert leidenschaftlich erregt worden durch das Eindringen
Aristotelischer Philosophie, in der Gestalt welche
ihr der Spanische Araber Ibn-Roschd (Averroës)
gegeben hatte, in die Behandlung theologischer
Fragen. Lange wurden die Averroisten als Ketzer verfolgt und noch in Fresken des vierzehnten
Jahrhunderts erscheint Averroës als typischer
Vertreter des Unglaubens; ihn aber betrachtete
man wieder als den Chorführer der Philosophen
jener Zeit. Erst bei den grossen Kirchenlehrern
der zweiten Hälfte des Jahrhunderts, bei Albert
von Cöln, Thomas von Aquino und Wilhelm Durantis, finden wir die peripatetische Philosophie
des Averroismus entkleidet, mit der Theologie
versöhnt und zur Hauptstütze scholastischer Begründung der Kirchenlehre umgestaltet. Wenn
nun auch durchaus nicht zu behaupten ist, dass
es gerade Averroistische Wege gewesen seyen,
welche Dante eingeschlagen, so hat es doch
durchaus nichts Befremdendes, dass die Wande-

lungen des Verhältnisses von Religion und Philosophie, welche jenes Jahrhundert erfahren, sich im Geiste des Dichters individuell wiederholt haben."

How deceptive the light of Philosophy is, and why it is so, Beatrice tells us in the *Paradiso* (xxix. 85) :—

> Voi non andate giù per un sentiero
> Filosofando, tanto vi trasporta
> L' amor dell' apparenza e' l suo pensiero.

Ye cannot walk on earth the sure and certain way
If led by Reason's lamp: so oft the love
Of visions false and fitful thought lead all astray.

The training which the poet has enjoyed in the school of the wisdom of the world, so far from helping, has only hindered him from realising the divine truths which Beatrice reveals to him.

Hence, to the question why her speech is so dark to him, she answers:—

> Perchè conoschi, disse, quella scuola
>   C' hai seguitata, e veggi sua dottrina
>   Come può seguitar la mia parola;
> E veggi vostra via dalla divina
>   Distar cotanto, quanto si discorda
>   Da terra il ciel che più alto festina.

That thou mayest know what kind of school
    It is thou followest, how such a doctrine
    Ne'er can understand my word or rule.
Thou seest too how far from the divine
    Thy way lies, far as from the earth
    The loftiest heaven, and the stars that shine!

Dante has become estranged from Christianity; he lacks the three virtues so characteristic of our faith; the bad passions which take their place drag him back to the stormy life where there is no light.

Then comes the Grace of God and revives the Ray of Religion; he repents having cherished the arrogance of philosophy; there is a resistless resurrection of the old faith, of the old love to Beatrice.

Contra questo avversario della ragione si levò un di, quasi nell'ora di nona, una forte immaginazione in me: chè mi parea vedere questa gloriosa Beatrice con quelle vestimenta saguigne, colle quali apparve prima agli occhi miei.—*Vita Nuova*, cap. 40.

On the day when the Saviour redeemed the human race, he too feels a mighty moving of the Spirit and experiences a great salvation. But, according to the Catholic Church, past sins still weigh upon the soul; so must the sinner's crushed and sin-laden heart experience the awfulness of its estrangement from God, and then, by expiation in Purgatory, become meet for the Paradise which God has prepared for spirits redeemed.

We have seen, then, that Portinari's daughter, who, on earth, had been for Dante the embodiment of a pure and lofty piety, becomes, as he returns to her in ideal revival after a period of unfaithfulness, a higher and altogether spiritual Beauty, a symbol of the deeper knowledge of God, of a theology refined and strengthened by science against doubt and false doctrine. Already in the *Vita Nuova* our poet had said:—

> Appresso a questo sonetto apparve a me una mirabil visione, nella quale vidi cose, che mi facero proporre di non dir più di questa benedetta, infino a tanto ch'io non potessi più degnamente trattare di lei E di venire a ciò io studio

quanto posso, sì com' ella sa veracemente. Sicchè, se piacere sarà di Colui per cui tutte le cose vivono, che la mia vita per alquanti anni perseveri, spero di dire di le quello che ma non fu detto d'alcuna.

It having pleased Him in whom all things live to spare the poet's life, he wrote in the *Comedy Divine* :—

O donna di virtù, sola per cui
    L'umana specie eccede ogni contento
    Da quel ciel che ha minor li cerchi sui.

O highly gifted lady, thee to know
    Enables man to rise, and to excel
    Whate'er the circles of the lower heaven
    show!
                          —*Inf.* ii. 76.

Veramente a così alto sospetto
    Non ti fermar, se quella nol ti dice
    Che lume fia tra il vero e l'intelletto.
Non so se intendi ; io dico di Beatrice :
    Tu la vedrai di sopra, in su la vetta
    Di questo monte, ridente e felice.

To such high questionings be thou no slave
    But list' to me until, at length, she come
    Who only from the depths of doubt can save,
Who is the light 'twixt intellect and truth.
    Beatrix call to mind; for, on this mountain's top
    Thou'lt see her, smiling, with the bloom of youth!
                          —*Purg.* vi. 43.

    O luce, o gloria della gente umana.

O light, O glory of the human race!
                          —*Purg.* xxxiii. 115.

O amanza del primo amante, o diva,
    Diss' io appresso, il cui parlar m' inonda
    E scalda si che più e più m'avviva.

Primæval Love's beloved, soul divine,
    Thy speech so warms and moves me, that I glow
    With love renewed and life that's more than mine!
                          —*Par.* vi. 118.

As to Dante's second love there can

be no doubt, for he tells us in the *Convivio* (ii. 16) :—

"Cosi, in fine di questo secondo trattato, dico ed affermo che la donna di cui io innamorai appresso lo primo amore, fu la bellissima ed onestissima figlia dello Imperadore dell' Universo alla quale Pitagora pose nome Filosofia."

Thus at the end of this second treatise I say and affirm, that the lady of whom I was enamored after the first love, was the most beautiful and honourable daughter of the Emperor of the Universe, to whom Pythagoras gave the name of Philosophy.

It seems that at this time our poet was engaged in reading the works of Cicero and Boëthius, who had often found comfort in Philosophy. Had not the former exclaimed ?—

"O vitæ philosophia dux! O virtûtis indagâtrix, expultrixque vitiôrum! quid non modo nos, sed omnîno vita hominum sine te esse potuisset?

Tu urbes peperisti; tu dissipâtos homines in societâtem vitæ convocasti."

"*O philosophy, guide of life. O searcher out of virtues and expeller of vices! What could we have done without thee: and not only we, but every age of man? It is thou that didst form cities; thou that didst call together solitary men to the enjoyment of social intercourse.*"

"E misimi a leggere quello libro di Boezio, nel quale, cattivo e discacciato, consolato s' avea, e un altro libro che Tullio scritto avea, nel quale, trattando dell' amistà, avea toccate parole della consolazione di Selio nella morte di Scipione amico suo. . . . Io, che cercava di consolare me trovai non solamente alle mie lagrime rimedio, ma vocaboli d' autori e di scienze e di libri, li quali considerando, giudicava bene, che la Filosofia, che era donna di questi autori, di queste scienze e di questi libri, fosse somma cosa. E immaginava lei falta come una *donna gentile*, e non la potea immaginare in alto alcuno se non misericordioso. E da questo immaginare cominciai ad andare là ov' ella si dimostrava veracemente, cioè nelle scuole de' religiosi, e alle disputazioni de' filosofanti; sicchè in picciol tempo, forse di trenta mesi, cominciai tanto a sentire della sua dolcezza, che 'l suo amore cacciava e distruggeva ogni altro pensiero. . . . Questa donna fu figlia d' Iddio, regina di tutto, nobilissima e bellissima Filosofia."

"*I set myself to read that book of Boëthius in which, though a captive and in exile, he found consolation, and another book which Cicero had written concerning* friendship, *wherein are the touching words of the consolation of Selius at the death of his friend Scipio. . . . I, who sought comfort, found not only a solace to my tears, but, weighing well the words of science and literature, it seemed to me that Philosophy, which was the bride of those two authors, was really the goal of all. I conceived it as a gentle lady, whom I could not imagine as anything but sympathetic. Her I followed in the schools of the religious and in speculative arguments, where she is best shown and known; so that in a short time, perhaps thirty months, I began to feel her sweetness to such an extent that her love concealed and destroyed every other thought. . . .*

And this was the daughter of the Lord, the queen of all, the most noble and beautiful Philosophy."

Her eyes, whose beauty the poet praises, are her *proofs;* by her smile she *persuades.* Love of her finds expression in earnest thought. Dante's philosophy is cognition and recognition of Truth, not however so much from an ethical as rather from a metaphysical standpoint. Metempirical questions are what chiefly interested our poet, and, at all events at first, seemed to offer him no insuperable difficulties. He fought hard for the conquest of knowledge; but the greater his exertions, the higher he climbed the cold and lonely heights of speculation, the farther from him in doubtful dimness seemed to gleam the star of Truth! At first philosophic investigation promised to give light, but the eye of the seeker soon became lost in gloom; the noble lady only hid herself in the thicker veil. Not that Dante had at all a low conception of Philosophy. "La Filosofia, in sè considerata, ha per suggetto lo intendere, e per forma un quasi divino amore allo intelletto." And the poet had honestly expected at once light and help at the shrine of this "gentle lady." Nevertheless, after passing through the eighth sphere of the physical and metaphysical sciences, ay, and even the ninth sphere of moral science, he is still in darkness and in doubt. Goethe somewhere says: "Der Kampf zwischen Christenthum und menschlicher Weisheit macht das Geheimniss der Weltgeschichte aus."

And this is exactly what Dante found. It was only when he entered the quiet heaven of the divine science, Theology, that he realised the peace and the joy of which he had so long been in search.

Ancora lo cielo empireo, per la sua pace, simiglia la *divina scienza,* che piena è di tutta pace, la quale non soffera lite alcuna d'opinioni o di sofistici argomenti, per la eccellentissima certezza del suo sogetto, lo quale è Iddio. E die questa dice Esso alli suoi discepoli " La pace mia do a voi, la pace mia lascio a voi," dando e lasciando loro la sua dottrina che i questa scienza di cui i parlo.—*Conv.* ii. 15.

At last, then, in the *Divine Comedy* Dante comes to a clear conviction that it is impossible for unaided human reason to arrive at the knowledge of eternal truths.

Matto è chi spera che nostra ragione
    Possa trascorrer la infinita via
    Che tiene una sustanzia in tre persone.

State contenti, umana gente, al *quia ;*
    Chì se potuto aveste veder tutto,
    Mestier non era partorir Maria.

E disiar vedeste senza frutto
    Tai, che sarebbe lor disio quetato,
    Ch' eternalmente è dato lor per lutto.

Io dico d'Aristotele e di Plato
    E di molti altri. E qui chinò la fronte,
    E più non disse, e rimase turbato.

That man is blind who hopes by human thought
    To cross the infinite, eternal way
    Which holds one substance in three persons, sought

By all. O man, suffice "so must it be";
    For if to men omniscience aye were given,
    What need of Mary, Virgin-Mother, we?

Those too, whose quest were ever vain
    If their desire forthwith were stilled,
    Which now they seek for ever to attain.

> *Of Aristotle, Plato, thus I speak,*
>   *Of many others too. The master said*
>   *No more, methought almost his heart would*
>   *break!*

Such, then, is "il poema sacro," this Comedy Divine, this Building beautiful and bold, erected by the hands of Heaven and of Earth!

This is the work of which Schelling said:—

"Es ist kein einzelnes Werk eines besondern Zeitalters, einer besondern Stufe der Bildung, sondern urbildlich durch die Allgemeingültigkeit, die es mit der absolutesten Individualität vereinigt, durch die Universalität, vermöge der es keine Seite des Lebens und der Bildung ausschliesst, durch die Form endlich, welche nicht besonderer Typus, sondern Typus der Betrachtung des Universums überhaupt ist."

In conclusion, let us not forget Dante's exquisite feeling for the Stars, the type and trope of Infinity. Each cantica ends with the word *stelle*. He issues forth from the Inferno *a riveder le stelle*, "to see again the stars." At the summit of the Purgatorio he feels *puro e disposto a salire alle stelle*, "pure and ready to mount unto the stars." Having attained the Paradiso, his will becomes one with the Divine Will, with *L'Amor che muove il Sole e l'altre stelle*, "Love that moveth Sun and Stars!" And what his old master Brunetto Latini said to him in the gloomy circle of Hell, the poet says to us to-day from Paradise :—

Se tu segui tua stella, non puoi fallire a glorioso porto.

"*Follow thou thy Star, thou shalt not fail of a glorious heaven!*"

Look to Christ, thou shalt not fail of Paradise!

APPENDIX.

In taking leave of our poet it may be well to remember one or two more of those exquisite inspirations which at once reveal the supreme artist. Dante is great, not only in what he said and sang, but also in what he left unsaid and unsung. Take, for instance, the way in which he deals with the three sublime Christian concepts: Faith, Hope, Love; the Vision of the Cross in the planet Mars; or the queenly figure of Fortune, the angel in disguise.

> Quest' è colei ch' è tanto posta in croce
>   Pur da color, che le dovrian dar lode,
>   Dandole biasmo a torto e mala voce.

Ma ella s' è beata, e ciò non ode:
Con l' altre prime creature lieta
Volve sua spera, e beata si gode.

And this is she who, though revilèd much
  (*Upon her laying shame and evil voice,*)
  By those e'en whom, of all, her love should touch,
Is blessed still, and wotteth not of this:
  With nature's other primal creatures' bliss
  Her sphere revolves, and cannot but rejoice!—*Inf.* vii. 91-96.

THE CROSS.

Qui vince la memoria mia lo ingegno;
  Chè in quella croce lampeggiava Cristo,
  Si ch' io non so trovare esemplo degno
Ma chi prende sua croce e segue Cristo,
  Ancor mi scuserà di quel ch' io lasso,
  Veggendo in quell' albór balenar Cristo.
Di corno in corno, e tra la cima e il basso,
  Si movean lumi, scintillando forte
  Nel congiungersi insieme e nel trapasso.
Così si veggion qui diritte e torte,
  Veloci e tarde, rinnovando vista,
  Le minuzie de' corpi, lunghe e corte,

Moversi per lo raggio, onde si lista
    Tal volta l' ombra, che per sua difesa
    La gente con ingegno ed arte acquista.
E come giga ed arpa in tempra tesa
    Di molte corde fan dolce tintinno
    A tal da cui la nota non è intesa;
Così da' lumi che lì m' apparinno
    S' accogliea per la croce una melode,
    Che mi rapiva senza intender l' inno.
Ben m' accors' io ch' ell' era d' alte lode,
    Perocchè a me venia *Risurgi e vinci*,
    Com' a colui che non intende, e ode.
                        —*Par.* xiv. 103-126.

*Here memory mocks the toil of genius. Christ
Beam'd on that Cross; and pattern fails me now,
But whoso takes his cross, and follows Christ,
Will pardon me for that I leave untold,
When in the fleckered dawning he shall spy
The glitterance of Christ. From horn to horn
And 'tween the summit and the base, did move
Lights, scintillating, as they met and pass'd.
That oft are seen, with ever-changeful glance,
Straight or athwart, now rapid and now slow,
The atomics of bodies, long or short,
To move along the sunbeam, whose slant line*

Checkers the shadow interposed by art
Against the noontide heat. And as the chime
Of minstrel music, dulcimer, and harp
With many strings, a pleasant dinning makes
To him who heareth not the distinct note;
So from the lights, which there appear'd to me,
Gather'd along the cross a melody,
That, indistinctly heard, with ravishment
Possess'd me. Yet I mark'd it was a hymn
Of lofty praises; for there came to me
" Arise," and " Conquer," as to one who hears
And comprehends not.
—(*Cary's translation.*)

FAITH.

Ed io rispondo: Credo in uno Dio
    Solo ed eterno, che tutto il ciel move,
    Non moto, con amore e con disio;
E a tal creder non ho io pur prove
    Fisice e metafisice, ma dalmi
    Anche la verità che quinci piove
Per Moisè, per profeti, e per salmi,
    Per l' evangelio, e per voi che scriveste,
    Poichè l' ardente Spirto vi fece almi;

> E credo in tre persone eterne, e queste
> Credo una essenzia sì una e sì trina,
> Che soffera congiunto *sunt et este.*
> —*Par.* xxiv. 130–141.

And I reply: I in one God believe;
One sole eternal Godhead, of whose love
All heaven is moved, himself unmoved the while.
Nor demonstration physical alone,
Or more intelligential and abstruse,
Persuades me to this faith: but from that truth
It cometh to me rather, which is shed
Through Moses; the rapt Prophets; and the
    Psalms;
The Gospel; and what ye yourselves did write,
When ye were gifted of the Holy Ghost.
In three eternal Persons I believe;
Essence threefold and one; mysterious league
Of union absolute.
—(*Cary's translation.*)

HOPE.

> Speme diss' io è uno attender certo
> Della gloria futura, il qual produce
> Grazia divina e precedente merto.

Da molte stelle mi vien questa luce;
   Ma quei la distillò nel mio cor pria,
   Che fu sommo cantor del sommo duce.
Sperino in te, nell' alta Teodia
   Dice, color che sanno il nome tuo:
   E chi nol sa, s' egli ha la fede mia?
Tu mi stillasti con lo stillar suo
   Nella pistola poi, sì ch'io son pieno,
   E in altrui vostra pioggia repluo.
                     —*Par.* xxv. 67–73.

       "*Hope*," said I,
"*Is of the joy to come a sure expectance,*
The effect of grace Divine and merit preceding.
This light from many a star, visits my heart;
But flow'd to me, the first, from him who sang
The song of the Supreme; himself supreme
Among his tuneful bréthren. '*Let all hope*
In thee,' *so spake his anthem,* '*who hath known*
Thy name'; *and, with my faith, who know not*
   that?
From thee, the next, distilling from his spring,
In thine epistle, fell on me the drops
So plenteously, that I on others shower
The influence of their dew."
                    —(*Cary's translation.*)

LOVE.

Lo Ben, che fa contenta questa Corte,
   Alfa ed Omega è di quanta scrittura
Mi legge amore o lievemente o forte.

   .   .   .   .

In this palace is the weal,
That Alpha and Omega is, to all
The lessons love can read me.

   .   .   .   .

Chè il bene, in quanto ben, come s' intende,
   Così accende amore, e tanto maggio,
Quanto più di bontate in sè comprende.

Good, inasmuch as we perceive the good,
Kindles our love ; and in degree the more,
As it comprises more of goodness in 't.

   Tutti quei morsi,
Che posson far lo cuor volger a Dio,
   Alla mia caritate son concorsi ;
Chè l' essere del mondo, e l' esser mio,
   La morte ch' el sostenne perch' io viva,
   E quel che spera ogni fedel, com' io,

> Con la predetta conoscenza viva,
>   Tratto m'hanno del mar dell' amor torto,
>   E del diritto m' han posto alla riva.
>
> —*Par.* xxvi.

> *All grappling bonds, that knit the heart to God,*
> *Confederate to make fast our charity.*
> *The being of the world ; and mine own being ;*
> *The death which He endured, that I should live ;*
> *And that, which all the faithful hope, as I do ;*
> *To the forementioned lively knowledge joined ;*
> *Have from the sea of ill love saved my bark,*
> *And on the coast secured it of the right.*
>
> —(*Cary's translation.*)

Lastly, in the next canto, Dante has given us the serene vision of Paradise in one matchless line:

> Ciò ch'io vedeva, mi sembrava un riso
>   Dell' universo.

> *And all I saw, seemed gathered up*
>   *In one World-Smile!*
>
> —*Par.* xxvii. 4.

Butler & Tanner, The Selwood Printing Works, Frome, and London.

www.ingramcontent.com/pod-product-compliance
Lightning Source LLC
Chambersburg PA
CBHW031401160426
43196CB00007B/853